We Can Vote

Voting Today

Voting A-K

Voting

Elise Wallace

We can learn.

We can talk.

We can listen.

We can watch.

We can think.

We can choose.

Think **and** Talk

How do people choose who to vote for?

We can help.

We can vote!

SIGN YOUR ENVELOPE & RETURN HERE

BALLOT DROP BOX

Jump into Fiction

Ann Votes

It is time to vote.
Ann thinks.

How will she vote?
Ann makes her choice.

Civics in Action

You can vote. First, talk and think. Listen and learn. It's okay to change your mind if you need to.

1. Hold a vote in your class for the best book.

2. Think about the best book you have read. Why is it the best?

3. Talk to other people. What do they think?

4. Vote on the class choice for best book.